My Confession of Faith & Praise!

A Handbook for Believers!

David Livingston J, M.E.

ISBN 978-93-5458-414-5
© David Livingston J, M.E. 2021
Published in India 2021 by Pencil

A brand of
One Point Six Technologies Pvt. Ltd.
123, Building J2, Shram Seva Premises,
Wadala Truck Terminal, Wadala (E)
Mumbai 400037, Maharashtra, INDIA
E connect@thepencilapp.com
W www.thepencilapp.com

Author biography

David Livingston J, a software professional turned academician, is doing God's ministry, especially in the form of writing Books and Tracts and distributing them to those who are in need.

He has been into teaching COMPUTER SCIENCE since 2003. He has expertise in Client/Server programming, Web programming and Enterprise computing.

He worked as an Assistant Professor in various Engineering Colleges affiliated to Anna University for 10 years. He also worked as HOD in the Department of Computer Engineering in SRI Polytechnic College, Coimbatore.

CONTENTS

Confession of our Faith in God!

A Breakfast Menu by Pearl Coleman!

Pearl Coleman

Really understanding what 'standing on the Word' meant altogether changed my life. Learning to put on the whole armor of God every morning that I opened my eyes with a "Good morning Father, Good morning Jesus, Good morning Holy Spirit" was a real step forward in my spiritual growth. Such a simple thing to do and so many Christians miss it.

Below are the words I speak out as part of my prayer time before I start the day. They are also given to many patients typed into an attractive picture frame.

Here is the breakfast menu to be read aloud to feed the spirit before feeding the body:

Good morning, Father! Good morning, Jesus! Good morning, Holy Spirit!

1. Heavenly Father, according to your Word, I present my body a living sacrifice, holy and acceptable in thy sight (Romans 12:1)

2. Upon Jesus I have built my life, my home and my future and the gates of hell shall not prevail against it (Matthew 16:18).

3. You are my Shepherd and I am your sheep. Therefore, I shall not want (Psalm 23:1).

4. You have supplied all my needs according to your riches in glory (Philippians 4: 19). And I cast all my cares upon you for you care for me (I Peter 5:7).

5. I cast down all imaginations and bring into captivity every evil thought, and I have the mind

of Christ (2 Corinthians 10:4, 5; I Corinthians 2:16).

6. You are my God who heals all my diseases and by your stripes I am healed (Isaiah 53:5).

7. I praise you and thank you for my prosperity and good health, even as my soul prospers (3 John 2).

8. The joy of the Lord is my strength (Nehemiah 8:10) and I can do all things through Christ which strengthens me (Philippians 4: 13).

9. Now, Heavenly Father, I praise you and I thank you for the armor you have provided for me to dress in this day. I gird my loins about with truth, I put on the breastplate of righteousness and I shoe my feet with the preparation of the gospel of peace (Ephesians 6: 13 - 15).

10. Above all, I take the shield of faith wherewith I shall be able to quench all the fiery darts of the wicked. Also I take the helmet of salvation and the sword of the spirit, which is the Word of God (Ephesians 6: 16, 17).

11. Now, I am completely covered in the name of Jesus, according to your word, Father. Moreover, the glory of the Lord is my rear guard (Isaiah 58:8)

12. Father, I have prayed according to your Word, and you have said you would watch over your Word to perform it (Jeremiah 1:12).

13. Father, just rise up and live big within me today, for I am yours. In the name of Jesus I Pray. Amen.

The Blessed Exchange by Ulf Ekman!

Ulf Ekman

At the cross,

- My debt was paid.

- The power of sin was broken.

- The power of sickness was broken.

- The power of poverty was broken.

- Enmity with God was broken.

1. Jesus died — so that I could have everlasting, abundant life, and enjoy fellowship with the Father as His child.

2. Jesus was made sin — so I could receive forgiveness and be made righteous.

3. "For He made Him who knew no sin to be sin for us, that we might become the righteousness of God in Him." (2 Corinthians 5:21)

4. Jesus took my sickness — so I, by His wounds, could be healed.

5. "But He was wounded for our transgressions, He was bruised for our iniquities; The chastisement for our peace was upon Him, and by His stripes we are healed." (Isaiah 53:5)

6. "Who Himself bore our sins in His own body on the tree, that we, having died to sins, might live for righteousness — by Whose stripes you were healed." (1 Peter 2:24)

7. Jesus became poor — so I, through His poverty, might be rich.

8. "For you know the grace of our Lord Jesus Christ, that though He was rich, yet for your sakes He became poor, that you through His poverty might become rich." (2 Corinthians 8:9)

9. Jesus took my anxiety — so I could have peace (Isaiah 53:5)

10. Jesus was made a curse — so I could be blessed.

11. "Christ has redeemed us from the curse of the law, having become a curse for us (for it is written, 'Cursed is everyone who hangs on a tree'), that the blessing of Abraham might come upon the Gentiles in Christ Jesus, that we might receive the promise of the Spirit through faith." (Galatians 3:13, 14)

My Position in Christ Jesus!

David Livingston J, the Author

I am a New Creation in Christ!

- I got circumcised when I came to Christ.

- I am set free from the spiritual powers of this world when I accepted Jesus as my Lord and Savior.

- I am forgiven and saved.

- "He has delivered us from the power of darkness and conveyed us into the kingdom of the Son of His love," (Colossians 1:13)

- I became dead and buried for sin when I was baptized.

- I am raised to new life with Christ.

- I am redeemed and bought with a price.

- I am stripped off my old sinful nature and all its wicked deeds.

- I am healed from all my diseases and I am hale and healthy now.

- "But He was wounded for our transgressions, He was bruised for our iniquities; The chastisement for our peace was upon Him, and by His stripes we are healed." (Isaiah 53:5)

- I am prosperous and successful in Christ. (Colossians 1:13)

- I am not forsaken but remembered by God Almighty.

- I am a beloved to God the Father.

- I am given eternal life to live with Christ forever.

I am a Hero of Faith in Christ!

1. Through faith, I understand the power of God in Creation. **"By faith we understand that the worlds were framed by the word of God, so that the things which are seen were not made of things which are visible."** (Hebrews 11:3)

2. I offer to God sacrifices that are pleasing and acceptable in His sight.

3. I walk with God and please Him in my day to day life.

4. I have come closer to God and whatever I ask in His name, I will get it.

5. I obey God and do all He wants me to do.

6. I get all the promises of God fulfilled in my life.

7. I receive all my blessings from God and will be a blessing to my future generation.

8. I hate the pleasures of this world and enjoy the company of God's children.

9. I am protected from all kinds of destruction and plagues.

10. I expect great things happening in my life such as walking through the Red sea and pulling down the walls of Jericho.

Amen!

My Never Again List by Don Gossett!

Don Gossett

- **Never again will I confess condemnation**, for "There is therefore now no condemnation to them which are in Christ Jesus" (Rom. 8:1). I am in Christ; therefore I am free from condemnation.

- **Never again will I confess bondage**, for "Where the Spirit of the Lord is, there is liberty" (2 Cor. 3:17); my body is the temple of the Holy Spirit (1 Cor. 6:19).

- **Never again will I confess supremacy of Satan over my life**, for "Greater is He that is in me, than he that is in the world" (I Jn. 4:4).

- **Never again will I confess lack**, for "My God shall supply all my needs according to His riches in glory in Christ Jesus" (Phil. 4:19).

- **Never again will I confess worries and frustrations**, for I am "Casting all my cares upon Him; for He cares for me" (I Peter 5:7). In Christ I am care-free!

- **Never again will I confess doubt and lack of faith**, for "God hath dealt to every man the measure of faith" (Rom. 12:3).

- **Never again will I confess fear**, for "God has not given me the spirit of fear; but of power, and of love, and of a sound mind" (2 Tim. 1:7).

- **Never again will I confess defeat**, for "God always causes me to triumph in Christ Jesus" (2 Cor. 2:14).

- **Never again will I confess lack of wisdom**, for "Christ Jesus, who of God is made unto me wisdom" (I Cor. 1:30).

- **Never again will I confess sickness**, for "With His stripes I am healed" (Is. 53:5); and Jesus "Himself took my infirmities, and bare my sickness" (Matt. 8:17).

- **Never again will I confess** "I can't," for "I can do all things through Christ which strengthens me" (Phil. 4:13).

- Never again will I confess weakness, for "The Lord is the strength of my life" (Ps. 27:1) and "The people that know their God shall be strong and do exploits" (Dan. 11:32).

Statement of Faith by Ian Andrews!

Ian Andrews

Here is a List of what I believe...

1. **I believe The Bible, both Old and New Testament**, to be the inspired Word of God, that it was given under the inspiration of the Holy

Spirit, that it is infallible and is the supreme authority in all matters of faith and conduct.

2. **I believe there is one living and true God**(manifested as Father, Son and Holy Spirit) infinitely perfect and eternal in existence. I believe God to be the Creator of all things and the Author of eternal redemption.

3. **I believe in the creation of man in God's image**, his fall through sin, his just condemnation to eternal punishment, and his need of personal salvation through repentance and faith in Jesus Christ.

4. **I believe in Lord Jesus Christ, who is the only and all-sufficient Savior.**I believe that Lord Jesus Christ to be God manifested in the flesh as the very Son of God – true God and true man, Creator of all things with the Father, and the appointed Judge of all men.

5. **I believe in the virgin birth of Jesus Christ, his vicarious death**on behalf of lost humanity, **his burial**, his **bodily resurrection**, his **ascension**on high, his High-Priestly ministry in the heavenlies.

6. **I believe in the Person of Holy Spirit**to change us into the likeness of Christ in thought, word and deed. I also believe in the baptism of the Holy Spirit subsequent to the New Birth; with the Biblical evidence of speaking with other tongues, with the endument of power to witness, with the

accompanying gifts, graces, and fruit of the Holy Spirit.

7. **I believe that Christ is the Head of the Church**which consists of all who have repented of their sins and confessed Christ as Lord and Savior in water baptism.

8. **I believe that the greatest commandment**for everyday Christian living is to love the Lord our God with all our heart, soul, mind, strength and to love others as ourselves (Mark 12:29-31).

9. **I believe that divine healing is part of the gift of salvation**, whether by the laying on of hands, the anointing with oil, prayer cloths, or by faith alone.

10. **I believe in the five fold ministries**and in the need for the Church to have biblical functioning of Apostles, Pastors, Prophets, Evangelists and Teachers within it so the body of Christ may be built up (Ephesians 4:11-13).

11. **I believe in the physical, personal, soon return of our Lord Jesus Christ**to earth to receive the righteous both living and dead, and to execute judgment upon the wicked (Acts 1:11; 1 Thessalonians 4:16-17; Titus 2:12-14; 2 Thessalonians 1:7-10).

12. **I believe in the resurrection of the dead**, the everlasting blessing of the saved, and the everlasting punishment of the lost.

Confession for Healing by Dodie Osteen! (Part I)

Dodie Osteen, the mother of Joel Osteen

"Praise the LORD, O my soul, and forget not all his benefits – Who forgives all your sins and heals all your diseases." (Psalm 103:2-3)

The healing scriptures that Dodie Osteen has stood on for over 25 years for healing are also listed in this booklet. She was diagnosed with cancer and told by her doctors to go home and prepare to die. Praise God she did not accept their diagnosis into her Spirit but ran to her Father and stood on His Word and promises. As a result, she was healed completely from cancer by the Grace of God and the Power of His Word.

1. **The Word of God will save my life**: "My son, give attention to my words; Incline your ear to my

sayings. Do not let them depart from your eyes; Keep them in the midst of your heart. For they are life to those who find them, and health to all their flesh" (Proverbs 4:20-22 NKJV)

2. **God's Word will not fail**: "Not a word failed of any good thing which the LORD had spoken to the house of Israel. All came to pass" (Joshua 21:45 NKJV)

3. **God's will — healing– is working in me**: "For it is God who works in you both to will and to do for His good pleasure" (Philippians 2:13 NKJV)

4. **The Spirit of Life is making my body alive**: "But if the Spirit of Him who raised Jesus from the dead dwells in you, He who raised Christ from the dead will also give life to your mortal bodies through His Spirit who dwells in you" (Romans 8:11 NKJV)

5. **God is for me**: "For all the promises of God in Him are Yes, and in Him Amen, to the glory of God through us" (2 Corinthians 1:20 NKJV)

6. **It is God's will for me to be healed**: "And behold, a leper came and worshipped Him, saying, 'Lord, if You are willing, You can make me clean.' Then Jesus put out His hand and touched him, saying, 'I am willing; be cleansed.' Immediately his leprosy was cleansed" (Matthew 8:2-3 NKJV)

7. **I will Obey God's Word to be healed**: "... If you diligently heed the voice of the LORD your God

and do what is right in His sight, give ear to His commandments and keep all His statutes, I will put none of the diseases on you which I have brought on the Egyptians. For I am the LORD who heals you." (Exodus 15:26 NKJV)

8. **I will Serve the Lord and healing will be mine**: "So you shall serve the LORD your God, and He will bless your bread and your water. And I will take sickness away from the midst of you." (Exodus 23:25 NKJV)

9. **God will take all sickness away from me**: "And the LORD will take away from you all sickness, and will afflict you with none of the terrible diseases of Egypt which you have known, but will lay them on all those who hate you." (Deuteronomy 7:15 NKJV)

10. **I will give God Tithe and Offering in order to be Blessed**: "Bring all the tithes into the storehouse, that there may be food in My house, and try Me now in this,' says the LORD of hosts, 'If I will not open for you the windows of heaven and pour out for you such blessing that there will not be room enough to receive it'" (Malachi 3:10 NKJV)

11. **One of God's benefits is healing**: "Bless the LORD, O my soul; And all that is within me, bless His holy name. Bless the LORD, O my soul, and forget not all His benefits: Who forgives all your iniquities, Who heals all your diseases, Who redeems your life from destruction, Who crowns

you with loving kindness and tender mercies, Who satisfies your mouth with good things, so that your youth is renewed like the eagle's." (Psalm 103:1-5 NKJV)

12. **God's Word brings healing to Me**: "He sent His word and healed them, and delivered them from their destructions." (Psalm 107:20 NKJV)

13. **God wants me to live**: "I shall not die, but live, and declare the works of the LORD." (Psalm 118:17 NKJV)

14. **I choose to live and fight a good fight!**"I call heaven and earth as witnesses today against you, that I have set before you life and death, blessing and cursing; therefore choose life, that both you and your descendants may live;" (Deuteronomy 30:19 NKJV)

15. **I will live a long life**: "With long life I will satisfy him, and show him My salvation." (Psalm 91:16 NKJV)

16. **Jesus bore my sins & my sicknesses**: "... He was wounded for our transgressions, He was bruised for our iniquities; The chastisement for our peace was upon Him, and by His stripes we are healed." (Isaiah 53:5 NKJV)

17. **God will restore my health**: "... 'I will restore health to you and heal you of your wounds,' says the LORD, 'Because they called you an outcast

saying: This is Zion; No one seeks her.'" (Jeremiah 30:17 NKJV)

18. **I take authority over the sickness in my body**: "Assuredly, I say to you, whatever you bind on earth will be bound in heaven, and whatever you loose on earth will be loosed in heaven." (Matthew 18:18 NKJV)

19. **I will agree with someone for my healing**: "Again I say to you that if two of you agree on earth concerning anything that they ask, it will be done for them by My Father in heaven" (Matthew 18:19 NKJV)

20. **What I say will make a difference**: "... Jesus answered and said to them, 'Have faith in God. For assuredly, I say to you, whoever says to this mountain, Be removed and be cast into the sea,' and does not doubt in his heart, but believes that those things he says will be done, he will have whatever he says." (Mark 11:22-23 NKJV)

Confession for Healing by Dodie Osteen!
(Part II)

Dodie Osteen with her husband John Osteen

1. **I Believe, and Receive**: "Therefore I say to you, whatever things you ask when you pray, believe that you receive them, and you will have them." (Mark 11:24 NKJV)

2. **I will Plead my case to God**: "Plead your case to God. I, even I, am He who blots out your transgressions for My own sake; And I will not remember your sins. Put Me in remembrance; Let us contend together; State your case, that you may be acquitted" (Isaiah 43:25-26 NKJV)

3. **I will have someone laying hands on me for healing**: "And these signs will follow those who believe: In My name they will cast out demons; they will speak with new tongues; they will take up serpents; and if they drink anything deadly, it will by no means hurt them; they will lay hands on the sick, and they will recover." (Mark 16:17-18 NKJV)

4. **I am a worshipper of God, Who heals me**: "Now we know that God does not hear sinners; but if anyone is a worshiper of God and does His will, He hears him" (John 9:31 NKJV)

5. **The devil wants to kill me; but God wants to heal me**: "The thief does not come except to steal, and to kill, and to destroy. I have come that they may have life, and that they may have it more abundantly" (John 10:10 NKJV)

6. **I am redeemed from the curse**: "Christ has redeemed us from the curse of the law, having

become a curse for us (for it is written, 'Cursed is everyone who hangs on a tree'), that the blessing of Abraham might come upon the Gentiles in Christ Jesus, that we might receive the promise of the Spirit through faith." (Galatians 3:13-14 NKJV)

7. **I will not waiver in my faith**: "Let us hold fast the confession of our hope without wavering, for He who promised is faithful" (Hebrews 10:23 NKJV)

8. **I have confidence in God and in His Word**: "Therefore do not cast away your confidence, which has great reward" (Hebrews 10:35 NKJV)

9. **I will find strength in God and in His Word**: ".… Let the weak say, 'I am strong.'" (Joel 3:10 NKJV)

10. **Jesus Christ has never changed; What He did 2000 years ago, He will do for me today**: "Jesus Christ is the same yesterday, today, and forever" (Hebrews 13:8 NKJV)

11. **God's highest wish for me is to be well**: "Beloved, I pray that you may prosper in all things and be in health, just as your soul prospers." (3 John 1:2 KJV)

12. **I will be anointed with oil by a Christian who believes in healing**: "Is anyone among you sick? Let him call for the elders of the church, and let them pray over him, anointing him with oil in the

name of the Lord. And the prayer of faith will save the sick, and the Lord will raise him up. And if he has committed sins, he will be forgiven" (James 5:14-15 NKJV)

13. **Jesus has already paid the price for my healing**: "Who Himself bore our sins in His own body on the tree, that we, having died to sins, might live for righteousness; by whose stripes you were healed" (1 Peter 2:24 NKJV)

14. **I will be confident in God, Who answers my prayers**: "Now this is the confidence that we have in Him, that if we ask anything according to His will, He hears us. And if we know that He hears us, whatever we ask, we know that we have the petitions that we have asked of Him" (1 John 5:14-15 NKJV)

15. **God answers my prayers because I keep His commandments**: "Beloved, if our heart does not condemn us, we have confidence toward God. And whatever we ask we receive from Him, because we keep His commandments and do those things that are pleasing in His sight" (1 John 3:21-22 NKJV)

16. **Fear is not of God, therefore I Rebuke it!** "For God has not given us a spirit of fear, but of power and of love and of a sound mind" (2 Timothy 1:7 NKJV)

17. **I will cast down those thoughts and imaginations that don't line up with the Word**

of God: "For the weapons of our warfare are not carnal but mighty in God for pulling down strongholds, casting down arguments and every high thing that exalts itself against the knowledge of God, bringing every thought into captivity to the obedience of Christ" (2 Corinthians 10:4-5 NKJV)

18. **I will be strong in the Lord's power**: "Finally, my brethren, be strong in the Lord and in the power of His might. Put on the whole armor of God, that you may be able to stand against the wiles of the devil. For we do not wrestle against flesh and blood, but against principalities, against powers, against the rulers of the darkness of this age, against spiritual hosts of wickedness in the heavenly places." (Ephesians 6:10-12 NKJV)

19. **I will give testimony of my healing**: "And they overcame him by the blood of the Lamb and by the word of their testimony, and they did not love their lives to the death" (Revelation 12:11 NKJV)

20. **My sickness will leave and not come back again**: "What do you conspire against the LORD? He will make an utter end of it. Affliction will not rise up a second time." (Nahum 1:9 NKJV)

Praise God of Trinity - Father, Son and Holy Spirit!

Knowing and Praising God of Trinity!

In the beginning God (Father, Son and the Holy Spirit) created the heavens and the earth. The earth was without form, and void; and darkness was on the face of the deep. And the Spirit of God was hovering over the face of the waters. (Genesis 1: 1, 2)

"Then God said, 'Let Us make man in Our image, according to Our likeness; let them have dominion over the fish of the sea, over the birds of the air, and over the cattle, over all the earth and over every creeping thing that creeps on the earth.' So God created man in His own image; in the image of God He created him; male and female He created them. (Genesis 1: 26, 27)

"And I will put enmity between you and the woman, and between your seed and her Seed; He (the Son of God) shall bruise your head, and you shall bruise His heel (God, the Son)." (Gen. 3:15)

"Then the Lord God said, 'Behold, the man has become like one of us (Father, Son and the Holy Spirit), to know good and evil. And now, lest he put out his hand and take also of the tree of life, and eat, and live forever.'" (Gen. 3:22)

Praise God the Father (Part I)

Praise God the Father, who is in Heaven

a. God, the Father revealed in Genesis:

1. God, the Father, You created me in your own image (Genesis 1:26, 27).
2. You are El-Eleon — God Most High, who created the heaven and the earth (Genesis 14:19, 22).
3. You are El-Shaddai — Lord God Almighty (Genesis 17:1; 35:11).
4. You are the Judge of all the earth (Genesis 18:25).
5. You are able to fulfill all your promises without fail (Genesis 21:1; 26:3; 46:3; 50:24).
6. You are with me wherever I go and whatever I do (Genesis 21:20; 26:24, 28, 29; 39:2, 3, 21, 23; 46:4).

7. You are the One who gives me success (Genesis 21:22; 24:12, 50; 39:3, 23).

8. You are El-Olam — God who exists for ever (Genesis 21:33).

9. You are Jehovah Jireh — the Provider (Genesis 22:14).

10. You are the One who blesses me richly (Genesis 24:35; 26:3, 12; 39:5, 26:24, 25:11; 30:30).

11. You are the One who prospers my journey (Genesis 24:21; 32:10).

12. You are the God of Abraham (Genesis 24:27; 26:24).

13. You are the One who shows steadfast love and faithfulness towards me (Genesis 24:27).

14. You are the One who leads me by the right way (Genesis 24:48).

15. You hear me when I call and answer my prayers (Genesis 25:21).

16. You know what will happen in the future (Genesis 25:23).

17. You keep me wherever I go (Genesis 28:15; 50:20).

b. God, the Father revealed in Exodus:

1. God, the Father, You revealed yourself to Moses as Jehovah (Self existing God — Exodus 3:13, 14; 6:2).

2. You are the God of Abraham, Isaac and Jacob (Exodus 3:15; 4:5).

3. You are the God of Hebrews (Exodus 3:18; 5:3).

4. You perform miracles by the power of your hand (Exodus 3:20).

5. You help me to find favour in the sight of others (Exodus 3:21).

6. You are the Creator of every man including blind, deaf and dumb (Exodus 4:11).

7. You teach me how to speak before my adversaries (Exodus 4:12).

8. You lead me and guide me in fulfilling your mission (Exodus 4:15).

9. You are the God of Israel (Exodus 5:1).

10. You are my deliverer (Exodus 6:6, 7).

c. God, the Father revealed in Leviticus:

1. God, the Father, You are holy (Leviticus 11:44, 45; 19:2; 21:8; 22:32).

2. You are the One who sanctifies me (Leviticus 21:8, 23; 22:9, 32).

d. God, the Father revealed in Psalms:

1. God, the Father, You are in heaven (Psalms 2:4; 14:2; 33:13, 14).

2. You are in your holy temple (Psalms 11:4).

3. You are good and upright (Psalms 25:8; 100:5).

4. You speak like thunder (Psalms 29:3-9).

5. You are awesome in your deeds (Psalms 66:3, 5).

6. You are worthy to be praised (Psalms 66:4).

7. You are Almighty (Psalms 91:1; 93:4).

8. You are upright (Psalms 92:14).

9. You are a great God and a great King above all gods (Psalms 95:3).

10. You speak even today (Psalms 95:8; 99:6, 7; 19:1-6).

11. You are great and exalted over all the peoples of the earth (Psalms 99:2; 95:3; 96:4).

12. You are holy (Psalms 99:5, 9).

13. You are unchanging (Psalms 102:12, 26, 27).

14. You are merciful and gracious (Psalms 103:8).

15. You are slow to anger and abounding in steadfast love (Psalms 103:8).

Praise God the Father (Part II)

Praise God in His Temple

a. God and Me according to Psalmist:

1. God, the Father, You are my Shepherd (Psalms 23:1; 100:3).
2. You are my rock (Psalms 62:2, 6).
3. You are my salvation (Psalms 62:2, 6).
4. You are my defense (Psalms 62:2, 6).
5. You are my glory and the rock of my salvation (Psalms

62:6).

6. You are my Creator (Psalms 95:6, 7; 96:5, 100:3).

7. You are my Upholder (Psalms 96:10).

8. You are my Judge (Psalms 96:10, 13).

9. You are my King (Psalms 99:1; 96:10, 97:1; 74:12).

10. You are my strength and my song (Psalm 118:14).

b. God is at Work in Heaven:

1. God, the Father, You speak to men from heaven (Exodus 20:1, 22; Psalms 2:5).

2. You are seated in the heavens and laugh (Psalms 2:4).

3. You get angry and terrify people in your fury (Psalms 2:5).

4. You set your chosen as King on the throne (Psalms 2:6).

5. You test the righteous, and the children of men (Psalms 11:4, 5).

6. You hate the wicked and the one who loves violence (Psalms 11:5).

7. You restore the fortunes of your people (Psalms 14:7).

8. You deal with me according to my righteousness and rewards me according to the cleanness of my hands (Psalms 18:20).

9. You look down from heaven and see all mankind (Psalms 33:13).

c. God, the Father revealed in Prophetical Books:

1. God, the Father, You are my Father (Isaiah 64:8).

2. You are the Maker of my soul (Jeremiah 38:16).

3. You are eternal (Habakkuk 1:12).

4. You are holy and pure (Habakkuk 1:12, 13).

5. You can not stand the sight of evil (Habakkuk 1:13).

6. You are in your holy temple (Habakkuk 2:20).

7. Your voice will roar from Zion and thunder from Jerusalem.

d. God, the Father revealed in New Testament:

1. God, the Father, You are on high (Luke 2:14).
2. You are unseen (John 1:18).
3. You are light (I John 1:5).
4. You are love (I John 4:8; John 3:16).
5. You are my provider (Matt 6:26, 30, 32; Romans 8:32; I Peter 5:7).
6. You exist from the beginning (I John 2:13, 14).
7. You are great and greater than anyone else on this earth (John 10:29).
8. You are good and perfect (Matthew 7:11, 5:45-48, 19:17).
9. You are the One who sent your Son in the likeness of sinful man.
10. You work for the good of those who love You.
11. You graciously give us all things for our living on earth.
12. You justify those who believe in You through Jesus Christ.
13. You make us more than conquerors through Christ.
14. You always cause me to triumph in Christ
(I Corinthians 15:17, II Corinthians 2:14).
15. You give me strength and make me shine like star (Philippians 2:14-16, 4:3).

e. God, the Father in Revelation:

1. God, the Father, You are Almighty (Rev. 1:8).
2. You are the Alpha and the Omega (Rev. 1:8).
3. You are the Lord, the God of the spirits of the prophets (Rev. 22:6).

Praise God the Son (Part I)

Praise God, the Son - Jesus Christ!

a. Pre Incarnate Jesus — Jesus appeared as an Angel:

1. Jesus, You appeared to Abraham in the land of Canaan (Genesis 12:7).
2. You appeared to Abraham in a vision (Genesis 15:1).
3. You appeared as LORD God to Abraham (Genesis 15:8; 18: 27, 30, 32).
4. You appeared to Abraham by the oaks of Mamre (Genesis 18:1).
5. You appeared to Abraham on the road towards Sodom

and Gomorrah (Genesis 18: 21 — 33).

6. You appeared to Hagar the Egyptian by a spring of water in the wilderness (Genesis 16: 7 — 13).

7. You appeared to king Abimelech in a dream by night (Gen. 20: 3, 4).

8. You appeared to Abraham as an angel on one of the mountains of Moriah (Genesis 22:11).

9. You appeared and spoke to Abraham from heaven (Genesis 22:15).

10. You appeared to Isaac in a vision by night (Genesis 26:2, 24).

11. You appeared to Jacob in a dream (Genesis 28:12 — 16).

12. You appeared to Jacob as an angel in a dream (Genesis 31: 11 — 13).

13. You appeared to Laban, the Aramean in a dream by night (Genesis 31:24).

14. You appeared as a man to Jacob and wrestled with him at the ford of the Jabbok (Genesis 32: 24 — 30).

15. You appeared to Jacob the second time in the land of Canaan (Genesis 35:9, 13).

16. You appeared to Jacob at Beersheba (Genesis 46:2, 3, 4).

17. You appeared to Moses in a bush (Exodus 3:2, 6; 4:24).

b. Jesus Christ, the Son of God:

1. Jesus, You are a person having equal status with God, the Father. Therefore, you are called the Son of God (I Timothy 2:6, 3:16).

2. You are God in a human form and You are the image of the invisible God.

3. You exist from the beginning and involved in creating

the world and everything in it.

4. You laid the foundations of the earth and made the heavens with your own hands.

5. You are unique (only one) - John 3:18, I Timothy 2:5, 6).

6. You are sanctified and sent by God, the Father (John 10:36).

7. You entered into this world from heaven (Hebrews 10:5).

8. You accepted a body for yourself to live on earth (Hebrews 10:5).

9. You submitted yourself to do the will of God, the Father (Hebrews 10:9).

10. You offered yourself as a sacrifice for our sins (Hebrews 10:10, 14).

11. You died for us and rose to life from the dead (Hebrews 9:28).

12. You are ruling the inhabitants of the earth from heaven.

13. You are going to come again to bring salvation to all who are eagerly waiting for you (Hebrew 10:37).

14. You are going to renew this heaven and earth.

15. You are the great God and Savior of all the earth (Titus 2:13).

Praise God the Son (Part II)

Praise God the Son, who hung on the Cross!

a. Jesus and Me:

1. Jesus, You are my Lord — Adonai (Genesis 15:1, 2, 8; 18:27, 30, 32; Exodus 4:10).

2. You are my Johovah (Psalms 80:17).

3. You are my Wonderful Counselor (Isaiah 9:6).

4. You are a Mighty God (Isaiah 9:6).

5. You are my Everlasting Father (Isaiah 9:6).

6. You are my Prince of Peace (Isaiah 9:6).

7. You are my Lord and my Savior (Psalms 2:4; 8: 1, 9; 68:19, 20; Isaiah 26:13, 14).

8. You are my Teacher and my Lord (John 13:13).

9. You are my Lord and my God (John 20:28; Acts 9:10).

b. Jesus, the High Priest:

1. Jesus, You are the Priest for ever (Hebrews 7:17, 21).
2. You are a Priest appointed by God after the order of Melchisedec (Psalms 110:4; Hebrews 7:17).
3. You are able to save all who come unto God by you (Hebrews 7:25).
4. You are holy (Hebrews 7:26).
5. You are harmless (Hebrews 7:26).
6. You are undefiled and separated from sinners (Hebrews 7:26).
7. You are made higher than the heavens (Hebrews 7:26).
8. You are seated at the right hand of God, the Father (Hebrews 8:1).
9. You are interceding for us as our great High Priest (Hebrews 8:1).

c. God, the Son in Revelation:

1. Jesus, You are the firstborn of the dead and the ruler of kings on earth (Rev. 1:5).
2. You are the One who is coming with the clouds (Rev. 1:7).
3. You are the first and the last, and the living one (Rev. 1:17, 18).
4. You died but alive forevermore (Rev. 1:18).
5. You have the keys of Death and Hades (Rev. 1:18).
6. You are clothed with a long robe and with a golden sash around your chest (Rev. 1:13).
7. Your hairs are white, like white wool, like snow (Rev. 1:14).
8. Your eyes are like a flame of fire (Rev. 1:14; 2:18).
9. Your feet are like burnished bronze, refined in a furnace

(Rev. 1:15; 2:18).

10. Your voice is like the roar of many waters (Rev. 1:15).

11. You hold seven stars in your right hand (Rev. 1:16).

12. You have a sharp two-edged sword in your mouth (Rev. 1:16).

13. Your face is like the sun shining in full strength (Rev. 1:16).

14. You are the Alpha and the Omega; the first and the last; the beginning and the end (Rev. 22:13).

15. You are the root and the descendant of David (Rev. 22:16).

16. You are the bright morning star (Rev. 22:16).

17. You are Lord (Rev. 22:20, 21).

Praise God, the Holy Spirit!

Praise God the Holy Spirit, who is with us always!

a. Truth about God, the Holy Spirit:

1. Holy Spirit, You are God and a part of the Trinity.
2. You are God sent to be with us by God, the Father and His Son Jesus Christ.
3. You exist from the beginning and live in the form of spirit.
4. You can descend and ascend like Jesus Christ.
5. Your personality is same as the personality of God, the Father and God, the Son.
6. You are the One who works here on earth on behalf of the Father and His Son Jesus Christ.
7. You are poured on mankind like water (Joel 2:28, 29;

Isaiah 44:3).

8. You are given as a Gift from God, the Father (Luke 11:13).

9. You have come from God, the Father to earth (John 16:8, 13).

b. Holy Spirit Speaks from the Beginning:

1. Holy Spirit, You speak audibly or through visions and dreams.

2. You spoke to Abraham (Genesis 12:1; 13:14 — 17; 22:1, 2).

3. You spoke to Rebeccah (Genesis 25:23).

4. You spoke to Jacob and gave him instructions (Genesis 35:1).

5. You spoke to Joseph through dreams and revealed his future (Genesis 37:5, 9).

6. You gave dreams to Cup bearer and Baker in the prison cell (Genesis 40:5).

7. You spoke to king Pharaoh in dreams (Genesis 41:1, 5).

8. You are the One who told Moses to return to Egypt (Exodus 4:19, 21).

9. You are the One who told Aaron to go and meet his brother Moses (Exodus 4:27).

10. You spoke to Samuel audibly (I Samuel 3:4, 6, 8, 10, 21).

11. You spoke to Peter through vision and audible voice when he was in the house of Simon, a tanner.

12. You spoke to Phillip and Ananias during the first Century A.D. (Acts 8:29; Acts 9:10-16).

c. Holy Spirit in the New Testament:

1. Holy Spirit, you can be heard and seen (For instance, John, the Baptist had seen the Holy Spirit in the form of a dove).
2. You are the Spirit of Truth, who leads me into all the truth.
3. You are the One, who convicts the people on earth of sin, righteousness and judgment.
4. You help us in my weaknesses (Romans 8:26).
5. You fill me and enable me to speak in unknown tongues (Acts 2:4).
6. You live in me (Romans 8:11).
7. You clothe me with power (Luke 24:49).
8. You empower me to do the work of God here on earth.
9. You strengthen me and make me a witness for God (Acts 1:8).
10. You intercede for me with groans that words can't express.
11. You lead me daily in my day to day life (Romans 8:14, 15).
12. You speak about the future and reveal the future (Acts 1:16).
13. You give me wisdom and revelation (Ephesians 1:17).
14. You fill me with joy (Acts 13:52).
15. You are the One, who prepares the church for the coming of the Lord Jesus Christ. Hallelujah!

www.ingramcontent.com/pod-product-compliance
Lightning Source LLC
La Vergne TN
LVHW041758190726
843493LV00008B/2693